World At Risk

RESOURCES

Andrew Solway

FRANKLIN WATTS
LONDON•SYDNEY

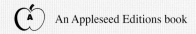 An Appleseed Editions book

First published in 2009 by Franklin Watts

Franklin Watts
338 Euston Road, London NW1 3BH

Franklin Watts Australia
Level 17/207 Kent St, Sydney, NSW 2000

© 2009 Appleseed Editions

Appleseed Editions Ltd
Well House, Friars Hill, Guestling, East Sussex TN35 4ET

Created by Q2AMedia
Editor: Michael Downey
Art Director: Rahul Dhiman
Designers: Harleen Mehta, Ritu Chopra
Picture Researcher: Shreya Sharma
Line Artist: Sibi N. Devasia
Colouring Artist: Aadil Ahmad, Mahender Kumar
Technical Artists: Abhideep Jha, Bibin Jose, Manoj Joshi

ISBN 978 0 7496 8813 4

Dewey classification: 333.72

All words in **bold** can be found in the glossary on pages 42–43.

Website information is correct at time of going to press. However, the publishers cannot
accept liability for any information or links found on third-party websites.

A CIP catalogue for this book is available from the British Library.

Picture credits
t=top b=bottom c=centre l=left r=right
Cover Images: Shutterstock: bg, Inset: Jan Van Broekhoven/shutterstock: cl, Desha/Shutterstock: c, Terrance Emerson/Shutterstock: cr

Russell Shively/Shutterstock: Title page, Ustyuzhanin Andrey Anatolyevitch/ Shutterstock: Content Page, Mike Norton/Shutterstock: 8,
Borer/Dreamstime: 9, Yvan/ Shutterstock: 10, Teun van den Dries/iStockphoto: 11, Bettmann/Corbis: 12, Neil Duncan/Photolibrary: 14,
Fedoro/Dreamstime: 15, Russell Shively/Shutterstock: 16, Frank Lane Picture Agency/Corbis: 17, Pichugin Dmitry/Shutterstock: 18-19,
Neil Duncan/Photolibrary: 21, Johanna Goodyear/Shutterstock: 22, NASA: 23, Nancy Marley/Argonne National Laboratory: 24,
NASA: 25, Roger Dale Calger/Shutterstock: 27, Kevin Schafer/Alamy: 28, Graham Prentice/Shutterstock: 29, Markross/Dreamstime: 30,
Joseph Luoman/iStockphoto: 31, Visuals Unlimited/Corbis: 32, Dana Ward/Shutterstock: 33, NOAA: 34, F.Bettex - Mysterra.org/Alamy:
35, Antonio Jorge Nunes/Shutterstock: 37, Mick Rock/Cephas Picture Library/Photolibrary: 38, Japan Travel Bureau/ Photolibrary: 39.

Q2AMedia Art Bank: 13, 18, 20, 26, 36, 40, 41.

Printed in China

Franklin Watts is a division of Hachette Children's Books,
an Hachette UK company.
www.hachette.co.uk

CONTENTS

1

GIFTS FROM THE PLANET

People rely heavily on the Earth's natural resources. Fossil fuels, trees and forests, fresh water and clean seas are all essential for life in our modern world.

Natural materials

To keep our industries working, our vehicles moving and our houses warm, we rely on the Earth's natural resources. **Fossil fuels**, for example, provide us with energy. To construct buildings we need metals and **minerals**, including iron and sand. All of these resources have to be dug up or extracted and then purified. They then have to be processed into materials that we can use.

Forests, such as this, are a rich natural resource. If looked after carefully, they could supply us with wood and other products for hundreds of years.

Air and water

Some resources are not as valuable as oil or metals, but they are just as essential for survival. Without water, there would be no life on the planet. Humans need to drink about 2 litres of water every single day to avoid becoming dehydrated. Equally important is the air we breathe. We cannot survive without air for more than a few minutes. Soil is another essential natural resource. We need soil to grow the farm crops and grass that feed farm animals. Without soil, people would starve.

Plants and animals

One other huge resource is the living things in this world. That is, the wide variety of animal and plant life that has developed on Earth. There are now millions of different kinds of wild animals and plants around the world. These help to shape and maintain the environment in which we live.

Squandering resources

As natural resources are precious, we should use them carefully or there will be none left for the future. However, this is not happening. Resources such as oil and natural gas are now being used up rapidly. When **reserves** are gone, there will be no more. Also, renewable resources, such as wood and water, are being used faster than they can be renewed. To make things worse, the way we produce and use natural resources is damaging the environment. Some scientists believe we are putting the world at risk if we carry on as we are.

Massive opencast mines are examples of the exploitation of resources. The quantity of resources available has decreased and the mining waste damages the environment.

9

2

FOSSIL FUELS

Oil, coal and natural gas are essential fuels that power the world's economies. Without these important resources, the modern industrial world would grind to a halt.

Swamp forests

Oil, coal and gas, often called fossil fuels, were formed from the remains of plants and animals that lived millions of years ago. Coal is the fossilised remains of massive swamp forests that flourished between 354 and 290 million years ago. Oil and gas formed more recently, between 160 and 10 million years ago, in the oceans. These fuels were formed from the remains of dead plants and animals that fell to the ocean floor and were buried under a layer of **sediment**. Over millions of years, heat and intense pressure turned the remains into oil and gas.

Oil is drilled from wells under the ocean from costly and dangerous drilling platforms.

Huge oil refineries convert crude oil into fuels and other useful products. They also produce **pollution** and waste that can damage the environment.

Fuel boom

Although coal has been used as a fuel for hundreds of years, oil and gas only became important in the early part of the 20th century. The biggest oil wells in the USA in 1900 were at Spindletop Hill in Texas. At the time, these wells produced 100,000 barrels of oil per day. This was more oil than all other wells in the USA put together.

The large amounts of oil extracted from wells at Spindletop Hill led to a boom in the use of oil, and later natural gas – oil and natural gas are often found together. At Spindletop Hill, however, the oil wells were almost dry after just two years of production. But the industrial boom fuelled by oil continued as oil fields were soon found in other parts of the USA and the world.

Running out

During the course of the 20th century, oil production has continued to grow at a frantic pace. In 1930, world oil production stood at about one billion barrels per year. By 2006, oil production had risen to nearly 30 billion barrels per year. But there is only a limited amount of oil in the ground.

No one knows exactly how much oil, gas and coal is left. The best estimate by scientists is that there are enough oil reserves to last for about a further 40 years at current levels of use. As demand for oil around the world is still rising relentlessly, the estimated reserves may last even less time than this. Natural gas supplies will last a little longer than 60 years. There is enough coal for another 146 years, although this may also change if demand rises.

Peak oil, high prices

Before the world begins to run out of oil, production will first reach a peak, referred to as 'peak oil'. This is the point at which we are extracting the maximum possible amount of oil each year from the world's oilfields. After this point is reached, the output of oil will gradually fall and we will have less and less oil each year to meet our rising energy needs. Many experts believe that we are now very close to peak oil production. Once production begins to fall, other energy sources will be needed urgently to replace oil. If we manage to make oil supplies last another 40 years, we will run out in around the year 2050. This means that in just 150 years, we will have used the Earth's entire reserves of oil. The graph on the opposite page shows how oil prices rose dramatically in the first few years of the 21st century as demand surged and the world moved closer towards peak oil.

Drilling for oil can cause serious pollution. When the Ixtoc I oil well burst in 1979, nearly half a million tonnes of crude oil spilled into the Gulf of Mexico. Today, it holds the record as the world's second largest ever oil spill.

Crude oil prices

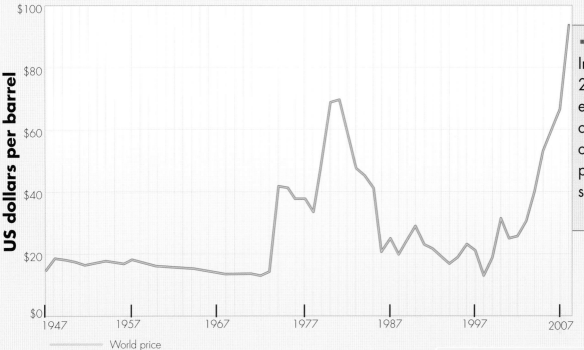

US dollars per barrel

World price

In the late 20th and early 21st centuries, crude oil prices rose steeply.

Floods, droughts and heat waves

When we burn fossil fuels for energy, we also release gases into the atmosphere that can be harmful in high quantities. One of these gases is carbon dioxide, which is sometimes referred to as a **greenhouse gas**. Once a massive amount of carbon dioxide has collected in the atmosphere, it acts to prevent the Sun's heat from escaping back into space after warming the Earth. Over the last 150 years, we have burned billions of tonnes of fossil fuels, releasing huge amounts of carbon dioxide into the atmosphere. It is now thought by many scientists that this massive amount of extra carbon dioxide is affecting the world's **climate** by causing temperatures to rise. In the future, this could lead to more floods, droughts and heat waves all around the world.

Polluting the planet

Spills from tankers and offshore oil rigs are not uncommon. Once in the water, crude oil damages natural **habitats**. It can take many years for an affected area to recover. **Sulphates** and **nitrates**, which are produced by the burning of fossil fuels, also pollute the planet. Once released, these substances dissolve into raindrops, making rain acidic. This **acid rain** can damage or kill animal and plant life, both on land and in the oceans. In cities and towns, acid rain causes damage to buildings, bridges and vehicles.

PLANET WATCH

» The largest ever oil spill occurred in 1991 during the first Gulf War. At least 780,000 tonnes of oil was spilled off the coast of Saudi Arabia. It caused an oil slick more than 160 km long and nearly 80 km wide.

» The world's worst tanker spill was from the Greek oil tanker *The Atlantic Empress*. In 1979, it collided with another tanker near Trinidad and Tobago, spilling out 276,000 tonnes of oil.

13

3 MINING

Nearly all the most important mineral resources, such as iron, clay, diamonds and uranium, come from the ground. Most of them are obtained through mining.

Big dig

Each year, the world's mining industries dig billions of tonnes of natural resources out of the ground. For every tonne of useful material mined, many tonnes of waste material have to be dug out. Iron ore may contain only 40 per cent of useful metal. The remaining 60 per cent is waste rock, or **spoil**. Manganese ore is about 70 per cent spoil, and many copper ores mined today are only 0.5 per cent copper and 99.5 per cent spoil. Gold is so precious that ore containing only 0.001 per cent gold is mined. It takes 100,000 tonnes of gold ore to produce 1 tonne of gold.

Earth Data

- On the Kola Peninsula in northern Russian, fumes from metal **smelting** have wiped out hundreds of square kilometres of forest. The destruction has created one of the largest man-made deserts in the world.

- Over a period of 100 years, metal mining and smelting around Sudbury, in Canada, acidified an estimated 7,000 lakes. It also killed thousands of trees over a huge area of about 17,000 sq. km.

- The South African mining industry is responsible for around a million tonnes of sulphur emissions a year. It is one of Africa's largest sources of acid rain pollution.

Despite the use of modern machinery and explosives, underground mining can be unpleasant and dangerous.

Opencast mines

Mining, and the large amounts of spoil produced, may destroy large areas of farmland, forest and wilderness. Opencast mining causes the most obvious damage. An opencast mine is one where the ore being mined is near the surface. Miners remove the layers of soil and rock lying over the ore deposit, then dig out the ore itself. As more and more of the ore is removed, the opencast mine becomes a huge hole in the ground. Around this hole are the huge quantities of rock and soil that are removed from the hole, and the waste produced from processing the ore.

Underground mines

In areas where mining takes place deep underground, there are no large holes on the surface. However, spoil from underground mines is brought to the surface and dumped in massive piles. As with opencast mining, the end result can be a **barren**, polluted landscape where the air is thick with dust and dirt.

Molten steel being poured at a steelworks. Steel makers rely on supplies of iron ore to make iron and then steel.

Spoil heaps

Over the past hundred years, about 100 million people around the world have had to move from their homes to make way for mining activities and to make space for vast spoil heaps. The South American town of Chuquicamata, in Chile, for example, was a town close to one of the biggest copper mines in the world. As the mine grew, it caused greater and greater amounts of pollution in Chuquicamata. The soil in the fields became heavily polluted with copper as well as with smaller amounts of highly **toxic** metals, such as arsenic and antimony. In 2002, the Chilean government decided that it was no longer safe for people to live in Chuquicamata. As a result, all of its inhabitants were moved to the town of Calama, 27 kilometres away.

> Chemicals washed out from mining wastes often seep into the **water table**, making fresh water in the area unfit for people to drink.

Toxic chemicals

The process of extracting metals and other materials from an ore can cause as much, if not more, pollution than the actual mining of the ore itself. Extraction often involves the use of highly toxic chemicals that stay in the mining spoil after the process is finished. Gold, for example, is extracted from very low quality ores using two processes. One involves the use of mercury, and the other the use of cyanide. Both of these substances are extremely toxic.

Poisoned rivers

There have been serious accidents where water polluted by the chemicals used in the extraction processes has escaped into the environment. In 2000, a leak at a Romanian gold mine led to 100 million litres of water **contaminated** with cyanide being released into the environment. The water found its way into the River Tisza, in Hungary, where it killed most of the plants, fish and animals that depended on the river.

The most beautiful rivers and streams can contain toxic chemicals that have seeped in from nearby mines and spoil heaps.

Exhausted mines

As with fossil fuels, there are limited supplies of iron, aluminium, salt and other materials in the world. Eventually, they will run out. But this will not happen for a long time as we have mined only a small proportion of this wealth in the Earth's crust. Although metals and minerals may not be running out, individual mines do run out of resources. In China, for example, 400 of the 8,000 working mines are exhausted and will soon close. New mines will then be opened. Every time a new mine opens, damage to the environment increases if land around an old mine is not restored.

Scarred landscape

Once a mine has been **worked out**, it is abandoned. In many cases, the scars created by the mining, and the piles of spoil, are never put right. These can continue to **blight** and contaminate the ground for years after the mine has closed. Chemicals from the spoil heap are washed into underground water supplies to pollute rivers, streams and drinking wells. Over time, this water pollution may affect large areas of land and its inhabitants.

Planet Watch

» In the past, mining was a difficult and extremely dangerous job. Between 1850 and 1930, 3,119 miners were killed in the UK's South Wales coalfield.

» Most modern mines are much safer. But in 2007, over 2,100 people still died in Chinese mines.

» Even in modern mines, accidents happen. In the USA in 2006, 13 miners died after an explosion in the Sago coal mine in West Virginia.

» In 2007, an explosion at the Ulyanovskaya coal mine in Russia killed 108 people.

4 SOIL

The thin layer of soil that lies on the surface of the Earth is one of our most vital resources. Without soil, we could not grow the crops essential to our survival.

Feeding the world

In the last 200 years, the world's population has grown at a faster rate than during any other period in history. In 1804, the world population was one billion. By 1999, the population had rocketed to six billion people. To feed this rapidly expanding population, large areas of land have had to be ploughed up to grow crops. Sophisticated and powerful farm machinery, along with artificial fertilisers and intensive livestock farming, have helped to increase the amount of food produced by farmers. However, this drive to produce more and more food is affecting the quality of the soil.

Earth Data

- Over 3,600 million hectares of land are badly affected by degradation. This is 25 per cent of the Earth's land area.

- Nearly one-third of the land used to grow crops has become unproductive in the last 40 years and has been abandoned. This is equal to 1,500 million hectares.

- It takes more than 500 years to restore just 2.5 cm of soil lost through erosion.

- **Pesticide** use has increased 50 times since 1950. Today, over 2.3 million tonnes are sprayed each year. However, less than 5 per cent of it actually kills pests and weeds. The rest badly pollutes the air, soil and water.

Land degradation is at its worst in areas where land is intensively farmed. This includes the wheat-producing areas of Europe, Asia and central USA.

Soil degradation around the world

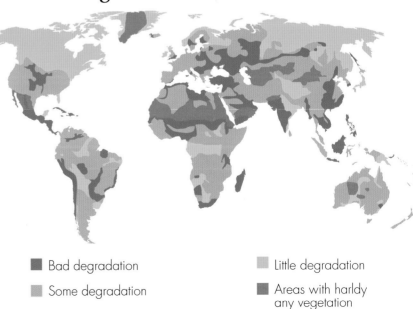

- Bad degradation
- Some degradation
- Little degradation
- Areas with harldy any vegetation

Unsustainable farming

Many modern farming methods are having a bad effect on the soil. After crops have been harvested, and there are no more plants to protect the soil from the weather, it is quickly **eroded** from fields by water and wind. Every year, about 2,500 million tonnes of topsoil is lost from the world's croplands in this way.

Although fertilisers and other chemicals make crops grow at a fast rate, they can also poison the ground if they are used over a long period of time. Salts and other harmful materials build up in the soil, while nourishing organic material that keeps the soil healthy is slowly destroyed. Heavy farm machines used to work the fields may also degrade the soil. Over time, the wheels of the machines compress the soil, pushing out the air. These air spaces in soil are essential for healthy plant growth.

Creating deserts

It is not just the growing of crops that damages soil. Animals can also cause serious damage. In areas with dry climates, herds of animals often **over-graze** pasture because there is not enough land. When most of the plants have been eaten, the dry soil is blown away and the area can become a desert. In the future, as **climate change** makes the planet warmer, the number of areas that become deserts is likely to increase.

When animals over-graze pasture land, grass is stripped away leaving the soil surface exposed. This eventually leads to erosion.

5 FRESH WATER

Water is essential to life. We use water for many purposes, from washing dishes to irrigating fields. But the amount of water we are using is draining the world's supply.

One per cent

On Earth, there is water almost everywhere. Over two-thirds of the Earth's surface is covered with water. Most of this water, however, cannot be used. Up to 97 per cent is salty ocean water, which is not suitable for drinking. Of the remaining three per cent, two per cent is locked up as ice in **glaciers** and ice-caps. Less than one per cent of all the water found on Earth is usable.

Availability of fresh water per person

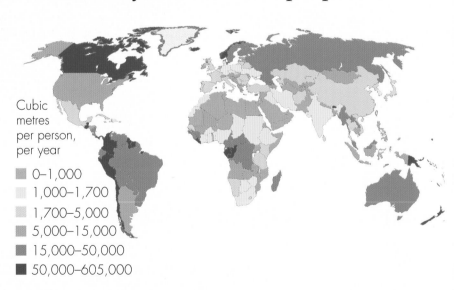

Cubic metres per person, per year

■ 0–1,000
■ 1,000–1,700
■ 1,700–5,000
■ 5,000–15,000
■ 15,000–50,000
■ 50,000–605,000

In recent years, a prolonged drought in several parts of Australia has forced farmers to rely heavily on irrigation to grow crops and to maintain pasture land for livestock.

Ground water

About 98 per cent of drinkable fresh water is ground water. This is water found below ground in porous rocks known as **aquifers**. Ground water percolates through rocks and eventually reaches the surface as a spring. However, it is known that water can also sink deep into the ground and then take thousands of years to return to the surface.

Springs are important water supplies not only for the rivers they feed, but also for people to tap into. We can also access ground water by sinking wells down into an aquifer, and pumping water up to the surface. The remaining 2 per cent of drinking water is found in rivers, streams and lakes.

Water shortage

In the world as a whole, there are about 34,000 cubic kilometres of fresh water available each year for people to use. If everyone had equal access to water, there would be enough for each person. In reality, water is not spread evenly. Large areas of the world are desert, while others receive heavy rain for a few months, followed by a dry season. In the rainy season, much of the water runs off into rivers and flows away. In the dry season, there are droughts and water shortages. Because of this, some areas are constantly short of water. It is estimated that 41 per cent of people live in areas where there is not enough water.

21

Major industries

Water is not just important for drinking; it is essential for domestic washing and cleaning. But much larger quantities of water are used by the world's major industries. Paper-making, for example, uses water to wash the paper pulp and make it into a liquid that will spread out into a smooth, thin layer. Many extraction processes in mining also use a lot of water.

Worldwide, the biggest use of water is for irrigation. In places where there is not enough rainfall, such as Africa and Australia, additional water has to be provided for crops to grow.

Water consumption

The amount of water people use varies greatly around the world. In less economically developed countries (**LEDCs**), people consume 60 to 100 litres of water per person per day. In more economically developed countries (**MEDCs**), each person uses almost ten times this amount. If we take into account the water used to irrigate farmland, the amount of water each person uses rises to between 2,000 and 5,000 litres per day in MEDCs. The amount of water we are taking from rivers, lakes and aquifers is putting a huge strain on the world's water supplies.

Many industrial processes would not be possible without the extensive use of water. This paper mill requires huge quantities of water to wash and prepare paper pulp for paper-making.

Gulf of California

When this photograph of the mouth of the Colorado River in the USA was taken in 2000, virtually no fresh water was flowing into the Gulf of California. The majority of the water had already been taken for irrigation and domestic use.

PLANET WATCH

» Each year, we discharge about 450 cubic km of sewage and other waste water into rivers, streams and lakes. Another 6,000 cubic km of water is then required to treat this sewage. In total, this is about two-thirds of all the world's usable fresh water runoff.

» Since 1972, countries in the eastern Mediterranean have been taking more water from rivers and ground water supplies than is being replaced by rainfall. Jordan and Yemen, for example, take 30 per cent more water from ground water supplies every year than is put back.

Dry wells

Today, people use about half of all the world's available fresh water each year. By 2025, this will rise to at least 70 per cent. Most of the world's large rivers are dammed in many places. In certain cases, this means that little or no water at all reaches the sea. In some regions where the water table has fallen, wells have dried up. In other areas, ground water has become salty. This is because there is so little water left in the aquifers that the salts dissolved in the water have become concentrated. As a result, many wells are no longer fit to use.

Unusable water

Pollution levels in ground water and in many rivers and lakes are so high that their water is unusable. Common kinds of pollution include toxic chemicals from leaking waste dumps and mine spoil heaps, and **pesticides** or **herbicides** that are sprayed on fields and then get washed into water supplies.

6

AIR

Human activities are polluting and damaging the air we breathe and the atmosphere that protects us from the deadly power of the Sun's rays.

Ultraviolet radiation

CFCs, or chlorofluorocarbons, are chemicals that were developed for use in aerosols and in refrigerators. Unfortunately, scientists found that when these CFCs escaped into the atmosphere, they damaged the **ozone** layer. What is the ozone layer? High in the atmosphere, between 10 and 50 km above the ground, is an area called the stratosphere. The ozone layer is a section of the stratosphere that contains a high-energy form of oxygen known as ozone. The ozone layer protects the Earth's surface from ultraviolet, or UV, radiation from the Sun's rays. Too much UV radiation can cause skin cancer, eye damage and other illnesses.

Earth Data

• The World Health Organisation estimates that 2.4 million people die each year from causes directly attributable to air pollution.

• In 1952, a thick, choking **smog** formed over London, and lasted for four days. The smog was a result of pollution caused by coal-burning fires. The Ministry of Health estimated that more than 4,000 people died as a result of the smog.

• Substances called **dioxins** are released into the air by certain manufacturing processes. The World Health Organisation wants our exposure to dioxins to be kept to an absolute minimum.

The haze over Mexico City is actually smog caused by ozone and other pollutants.

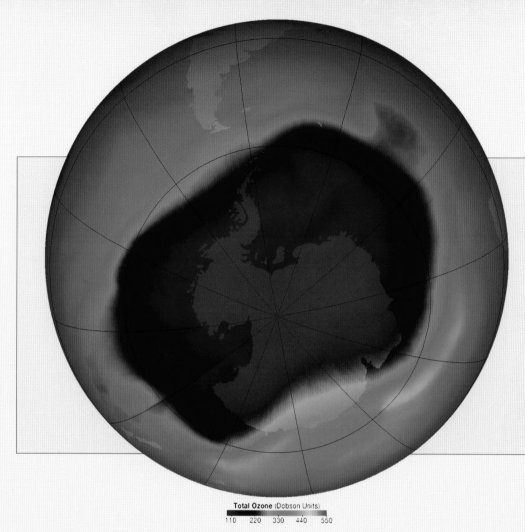

Total Ozone (Dobson Units)
110   220   330   440   550

The ozone layer is at its thinnest over the North and South poles. It disappears altogether over the Antarctic in summer. This leaves a hole, as the blue area in this photograph from 2006 shows.

CFCs have gradually damaged and broken down the ozone in the stratosphere. As a result, the ozone layer has become a great deal thinner. In some areas, ozone has been removed altogether, leaving a huge 'hole' in the atmosphere. Today, CFCs are generally not used in MEDCs. However, they are still widely used in LEDCs. This is continuing to damage the ozone layer.

Choking smog

Although ozone in the stratosphere is beneficial and protects us from harmful ultraviolet radiation, at ground level it is a toxic pollutant. Ozone is produced on the ground when gases from car exhausts or from factories are exposed to sunlight. The choking smog that forms in many cities on hot summer days is the result of ozone formation.

This ozone irritates the eyes and lungs, and can set off **asthma** attacks in **vulnerable** people. In the longer term, it can be serious and cause permanent lung damage and even early death.

Dangerous dioxins

Dioxins are chemicals that are released when substances that contain chlorine are burned. The biggest sources of dioxins are incinerators that burn household waste, and factories making fertilisers and other chemicals.

Dioxins can be harmful to health, even in tiny quantities. Research by the World Health Organisation has shown that people exposed to dioxins are more at risk of developing various types of cancer. Exposure to dioxins may also increase the risk of **diabetes** and other illnesses.

PLANTS AND ANIMALS

One of the Earth's most important resources is its huge variety of plants and animals. Human activities, however, are wiping out individual species at an alarming rate.

Natural substances

Living things and the health of planet Earth are firmly linked. Plants pump precious oxygen into the atmosphere. Without this oxygen, land animals could not survive. **Microbes** break down natural wastes and dead material, enriching the soil. Humans rely on other living things to provide them with food, building materials, clothing and many important medicines.

Earth Data

• Since 1970, there has been a 30 per cent decline in the number of different **species** in the world. Some 27,000 species are lost every year, which is three every hour.

• Every year, the International Union for Conservation of Nature publishes a Red List of endangered animals and plants. In 2007, 16,309 of the 41,415 species studied were under threat.

• 1 in 4 mammals, 1 in 8 birds and 1 in 3 amphibians are at risk of extinction.

• Up to 70 per cent of the plants on the 2007 Red List are under severe threat.

Plants and animals form complex food webs, showing that all life on our planet is interdependent .

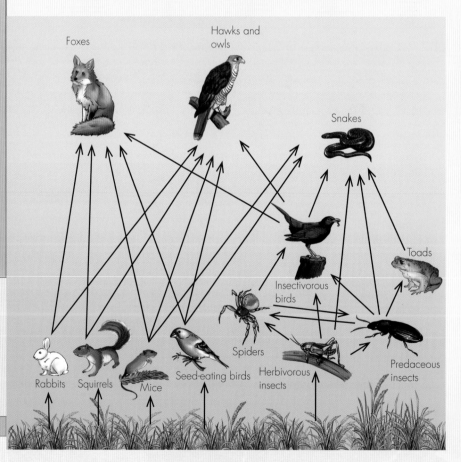

Foxes

Hawks and owls

Snakes

Toads

Insectivorous birds

Spiders

Seed-eating birds

Herbivorous insects

Predaceous insects

Rabbits Squirrels Mice

Cooperation and competition

A group of animals and plants that live together in balance with each other and with their habitat is called an **ecosystem**. Animals that live together in an ecosystem rely on each other in many ways. Several species of animal, for instance, may feed on the same plant, or on another animal. Sometimes, competition between species may cause some less successful species to move to another ecosystem where they may fit in better and thrive. Ecosystems as a whole are highly adaptable and can take challenging conditions in their stride. **Biodiversity**, or the rich variety of living things in an ecosystem, is the key to this ability to adapt.

Disappearing species

Many human activities are now reducing biodiversity. This is causing ecosystems around the world that once thrived to be put under threat. Animal and plant species are disappearing fast. Studies have shown that species are becoming extinct, or dying out, 50 to 100 times faster than the average extinction rate in the past. Predictions for the future are even worse. Scientists predict that by the year 2030, the extinction rate could be a staggering 10,000 times faster than the average extinction rate in the past. Already, 40 per cent of all remaining organisms on Earth are on the endangered species list.

Species such as the gorilla, the tiger and the rhinoceros are in danger from illegal hunting. Gorillas are hunted as exotic 'bush meat', while tiger and rhinoceros body parts are still used as ingredients in some traditional medicines.

Habitat loss

The loss of natural habitats for animals and plants has had the greatest impact on biodiversity. In 1700, three to four million square kilometres of land was farmed for crops. Today, more than 18 million square kilometres of land is cultivated. Over the same period, grazing land expanded from 5 million to 31 million square kilometres. This is a huge increase in the amount of land used for farming. Habitats have also been destroyed to make space for cities, towns, roads, railways, mines and factories. But habitat loss does not always mean the complete destruction of natural habitats. Sometimes, an ecosystem is broken up into small, poorly connected patches of land. This breaking up, or 'fragmentation', is almost as damaging as complete destruction. Each fragment of land can only support a small population of animals and plants, and it is usually difficult for animals to find their way to other fragments to find a mate to breed.

Soil pollution

Pollution can destroy living things in different ways. Pollution of the soil from mine waste, for example, causes toxic chemicals to build up in plants that grow in this soil. Any animals that eat these plants may well die or be badly affected. Pollution from fertilisers can kill wildlife in a section of a river or in a lake. Acid rain and other forms of air pollution kill or damage many forest trees.

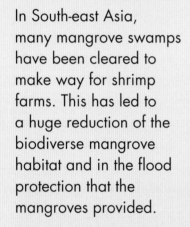

In South-east Asia, many mangrove swamps have been cleared to make way for shrimp farms. This has led to a huge reduction of the biodiverse mangrove habitat and in the flood protection that the mangroves provided.

Before Europeans came to New Zealand, there were almost no mammals. Mammals such as rats and cats have now killed off many native bird species. The takahe, shown here, is a native flightless bird that is critically endangered.

PLANET WATCH

» The Nile perch, a fish that has been introduced into the lakes of East Africa, has caused the extinction, or near-extinction, of several hundred native fish species.

» The water hyacinth, a plant from South America, has been introduced into North America, Asia, Australia and Africa. It forms dense colonies that block sunlight, clog water intakes and crowd out native species.

» Poisonous cane toads, introduced into Australia from Hawaii, have spread across the country in large numbers, displacing native species. Their poison kills predators that eat them.

Hunting and fishing

In the past, many animals were hunted to extinction. These include the passenger pigeon in the USA and the Tasmanian tiger in Australia. Today, although many species are protected from over-hunting, they are often hunted illegally. In the oceans, over-fishing has greatly reduced the stocks of fish such as cod and dory.

Invasive species

Another way humans have damaged natural habitats is by releasing animal or plant species into a new environment where they do not belong. The result can be very damaging to an ecosystem. In 1859, for example, 24 rabbits were released into the wild in southern Australia. By 1869, hunters were killing two million rabbits per year but were still failing to keep their numbers down. Today, rabbits have displaced many native animals from their habitats and are the cause of massive damage to crops.

8 FORESTS

For thousands of years, we have been cutting down trees for wood and for farming land. Today, this activity is endangering the habitats of many forest species.

Breathing forests

Rainforests are often called the 'lungs' of our planet. This is because they provide about 40 per cent of the oxygen produced by plants in the world as a whole. Plants in rainforests also absorb huge amounts of carbon dioxide from the atmosphere. Tropical rainforests, which are home to nearly 70 per cent of all plant species, are probably the most important of all the land habitats.

Around a quarter of all our medicines come from the plants that flourish in rainforests. Curare, for example, comes from a rainforest plant and was once used as a poison on arrow tips. Now, however, curare is used to relax muscles during surgery, and to help people with **multiple sclerosis** and **Parkinson's disease**.

The world's forests are a natural habitat for a huge and diverse range of life forms, from small plants to large animals.

30

Rapid deforestation

Despite the importance of these valuable resources, humans are destroying rainforests and other types of forest at an alarming rate. About half of all the world's mature rainforests have already been cut down. In many parts of South-east Asia, so much rainforest has been destroyed that the remaining areas are badly fragmented. Huge areas of conifer forests in northern Russia have also been cut down. Despite conservation attempts, deforestation is actually increasing rather than being reduced.

Officially protected

Wood for timber is the most common reason for deforestation. Tropical hardwoods are very valuable, so logging often happens illegally in areas that are officially protected. Soft woods, such as pine, fir and spruce, are widely used for paper-making. Trees for making paper often come from plantations where trees are replaced after they

> Once trees in a forest have been cut down, the top soil rapidly erodes. This then leaves very poor soil in which the forest cannot be re-grown.

have been cut down. However, the way the trees are grown on plantations allows for very little biodiversity in these artificial forests.

Single crops

In LEDCs, poor farmers often clear forests by burning to make way for the creation of small farms. The farms are only productive for a short time, but it takes many years for the forest to grow again. Forests are also cleared to make way for roads and settlements. In tropical areas, forests are cleared for plantations of single crops, such as rubber, cocoa or palm oil. All these activities are gradually eating away at the remaining rainforest.

9 OCEANS

More than two-thirds of the Earth's surface is covered by oceans. These vast watery regions are home to up to 90 per cent of all of our planet's living things.

Renewing the air

The surface of the ocean is full of tiny, plant-like organisms known as **phytoplankton**. These microbes make their own food through **photosynthesis**. During this process, phytoplankton absorb carbon dioxide and release oxygen into the air. Globally, around half of all oxygen produced by photosynthesis comes from these tiny creatures. Half the total carbon dioxide that humans have produced in the past 150 years has been absorbed by the oceans. Global warming, which affects phytoplankton, may reduce the ocean's capacity to absorb carbon dioxide over the next century.

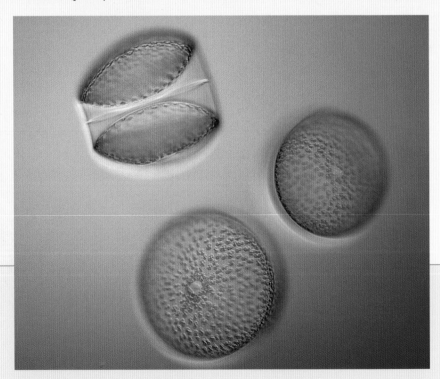

Phytoplankton are water organisms that play a vital role in absorbing carbon dioxide from the atmosphere.

This traditional Vietnamese fishing boat causes far less damage to ocean ecosystems than many modern trawlers.

Ocean ecosystems

A large amount of the pollution and waste that humans produce eventually ends up in the oceans. These pollutants have caused a great deal of damage to ocean ecosystems. Some of the worst damage has been to coral reefs, which are perhaps the richest, most diverse habitats in the ocean.

Coral reefs

Corals are tiny animals with a hard outer skeleton that live in large colonies in warm, shallow seas.

Close to a million different species live in the habitat created by the corals. Nearly two-thirds of the world's coral reefs have been damaged by human activities. Pollutants such as sewage and pesticides damage or kill the corals. The corals are dug out for building materials, and tourists take away pieces of coral as souvenirs. Some fishermen set off explosives in the water to stun fish, and this destroys large areas of coral. Reefs have also been damaged by climate change as, in some areas, the sea has become too warm for coral to survive.

Rich in food

We get huge amounts of food from the sea without having to plant crops or raise animals. Worldwide, we harvest more than 90 million tonnes of fish and shellfish each year. This is more than the total production of cattle, sheep, poultry and eggs.

However, we are now **over-exploiting** the ocean's fish stocks. We are taking more fish from the oceans than can be replaced by natural processes. Only 25 per cent of the fish species we eat are still in plentiful supply. The remaining 75 per cent are either being fished to their limit or are declining in numbers. Yet, as the human population grows, demand for fish will rise.

When corals are stressed, for instance by pollution or high temperatures, they 'bleach'. In other words, they turn white. Large areas of the Great Barrier Reef in Australia were bleached in 1998 and 2002. Some areas recovered. But in others, 90 per cent of the corals died.

Fish at risk

Over-fishing has had a disastrous effect on some ocean species. The almost complete loss of cod on the Grand Banks off the coast of Newfoundland, Canada, is a sad example. The Grand Banks have been rich fishing grounds for hundreds of years. However, in the latter part of the 20th century, fishing fleets began to take more and more fish.

By the 1970s, cod numbers on the Grand Banks had been drastically reduced. Although the Canadian government passed laws to ban foreign fishing boats, large numbers of cod were still caught. In the 1980s, scientists reported that fish stocks were at risk of collapsing. The government set limits on how many fish could be caught, but the **quotas** were too high. In 1992, numbers of cod suddenly collapsed to about 1 per cent of the

levels in the 1960s. In 1994, fishing for cod on the Grand Banks was banned altogether. Despite the ban, the cod populations on the Grand Banks have not recovered, and may never do so.

Fishing damage

As well as catching too many fish, modern fishing methods damage ocean ecosystems. Some fishing boats set out fine drift nets that are many kilometres long. Many marine animals are unintentionally caught in these drift nets and are killed when the nets are hauled in. Long-line fishing boats fish the oceans using lines with thousands of hooks on them. Often, large predator fish try to eat fish caught on the long line, and are themselves caught and die. Millions of dolphins have been accidentally killed in this way. Trawlers that drag huge fishing nets along the sea bed have damaged ocean ecosystems deeper down.

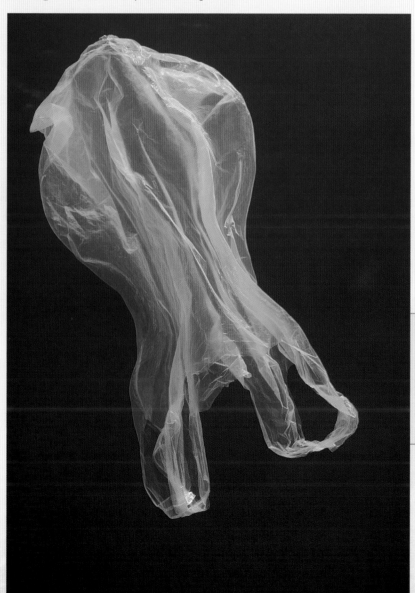

PLANET WATCH

» In some areas, pollution has led to the growth of large numbers of poisonous algae, which kill fish and other marine life. They create 'dead zones', where hardly any life can survive.

» Plastic waste dumped at sea is causing problems for marine life. For example, millions of tonnes of waste plastic have collected in an area of the Pacific Ocean that is known as the Great Garbage Patch. Here, marine animals eat the plastic thinking it is food, then get ill or die.

Plastic bags look similar to jellyfish, and sea turtles often try to eat them. This can cause illness and sometimes death.

10 SOLUTIONS

Human activities have put a great many of the Earth's natural resources at risk. We need to act now to save both our vital resources and the world as we know it.

Fewer people?

One of the main reasons for the strain on the Earth's resources is the growth in the total number of people. Controlling population growth, therefore, would be a big step in lowering our use of resources. In MEDCs, populations are stable, or even falling. Rapid population growth is taking place in LEDCs. The two most populated countries in the world, India and China, have expanded quickly in the past 50 years. However, both countries have succeeded in slowing this growth. Even so, the population in each country will continue to grow until 2030.

Earth Data

- Over the next 25 years, the global population is expected to grow to over 8 billion.

- By the year 2100, Africa is expected to become the continent with the largest population.

- The United Nation's Framework Convention on Climate Change agreed in 2007 that, by the end of 2009, they would work out a 'road map' for rapidly reducing **carbon emissions** over the following 11 years.

- In 2007, the European Union put in place laws that should reduce harmful carbon emissions from new cars by 19 per cent by the year 2012.

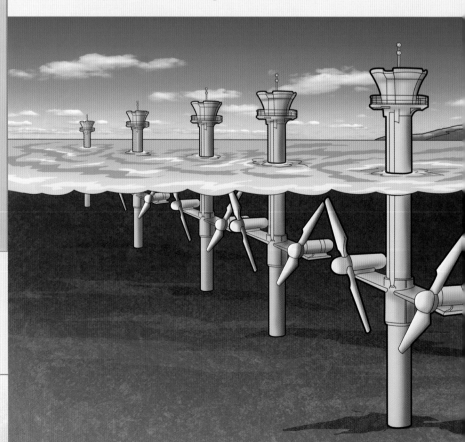

The tidal stream generator is being studied as an alternative source of energy.

Extensive research is being conducted to discover the best possible way to regenerate the rainforests and the diverse ecosystems that they sustain.

Energy needs

Although only a sixth of the world's population lives in the most economically developed countries, this sixth uses about half of the world's energy and other resources. If people in MEDCs could reduce the amount of energy and resources they use, this would greatly reduce the heavy strain that is being imposed on our world's valuable resources.

Improving insulation

How we heat and insulate our buildings is an important area of energy use. Many buildings are very inefficient and wasteful of energy. Governments in many countries are beginning to recognise this, and to encourage the construction

of new buildings that are more energy efficient. It is also possible to reduce the energy use of older, existing buildings. There are many ways of doing this, including improved wall and roof insulation and windows and doors that let less heat escape. New, energy-efficient appliances, such as cookers and refrigerators, can also reduce the amount of energy we use in our homes.

Recycling materials

Another way of using fewer resources is to reuse or recycle materials. Metals, such as steel and aluminium, can be recycled relatively easily. Recycling these materials uses 95 per cent less energy than making them from scratch.

Cleaner energy

The natural resources that present the most urgent problem are fossil fuels. We rely heavily on fossil fuels, and yet they cause climate change and will soon run out sooner or later.

Many other types of energy resources are being developed to replace fossil fuels. Each one has strengths and weaknesses. **Hydroelectricity** and nuclear power are already widely used for generating electricity. Solar power, wind power, tidal power, wave power and biofuels are all used to a limited extent and need to be developed further. Solar power and wind power are forms of energy that will not run out and do not produce carbon dioxide. Their main drawback is that they cannot provide energy continuously. Tidal and wave power are promising sources of energy, but as yet they have not been widely developed.

Fuel from waste

Biofuels are fuels similar to petrol, diesel and other oil-based fuels, but are made from plant oils rather than from petroleum. **Bioethanol**, made from sugar cane, is now used as a substitute for petrol in Brazil. Bioethanol made from corn is being used in the USA, while in Europe, biodiesel made from oilseed rape is being developed. However, all of these fuels are made from crops that are grown on

Drip irrigation, shown here, requires much less water than conventional irrigation. It also uses water more efficiently as water is slowly dripped directly on to plant roots.

Curitiba in Brazil is one of the world's most pleasant and well-planned cities that was designed for sustainable living.

land that could be used to grow food. This is not a good idea in the long term, since we will need as much space as possible for growing crops if the population continues to grow. However, newer biofuels are now being developed that are made from household waste, sewage, or from plants such as **switchgrass** that can grow on land that is not suitable for growing farm crops.

Sustainable development

There are many other changes that we will need to make if we want to preserve the Earth's resources for future generations. We need to avoid further deforestation, and find ways to preserve the remaining ecosystems and restore their richness. This is possible with a combination of science, technology and a change in people's lifestyles. We need to develop ways of living that are sustainable, that can be continued indefinitely without damaging the environment. Most of the science and technology we need for sustainable living is already available. The big challenge is to change people's attitudes and lifestyles.

PLANET WATCH

» Dongtan is an 'eco-city' for 500,000 people that is being built on an island close to Shanghai in China.

» The city is planned so that people will live close to where they work. People will therefore not need to use cars or other vehicles to get to work.

» Solar panels and small wind turbines on the buildings, and larger wind turbines outside the main city, will provide some of the electricity for the city. The rest will come from a power plant burning rice husks.

FACTS AND FIGURES

Fossil fuels and mining

	Resource	Amount produced per year	
		million tonnes	billion square metres
1	Coal	6,189	
2	Petroleum (crude oil)	3,889	
3	Natural gas		2,960
4	Iron ore	1,610	
5	Salt	256	
6	Bauxite (aluminium ore)	192	
7	Phosphate rock [1]	151	
8	Gypsum [2]	143	
9	Sulphur (recovered) [3]	62	
10	Manganese ore [4]	31	

This table shows the top ten resources produced from mining or underground drilling. We extract far more fossil fuels and iron than any other resource.

1. Used to make fertilisers.
2. Main uses are in plaster, fertilisers and some types of cement.
3. Used for making sulphuric acid and other chemicals. Also used for hardening rubber, such as for car tyres.
4. Used in steelmaking and as an additive to petrol.

Fresh water availability around the world

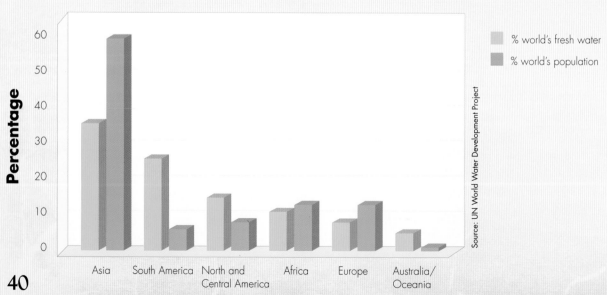

Source: UN World Water Development Project

Plants and animals

According to the World Wildlife Fund (WWF), the top ten most
endangered species are as follows.

	Species	Status
1	Black rhino	90 per cent drop since 1970. Fewer than 3,000 left
2	Giant panda	Fewer than 1,000 left in their native habitat in China
3	Bengal tiger	Poached for bones and body parts. Fewer than 6,000 remaining
4	Beluga sturgeon	Found mainly in Caspian Sea. Numbers have dropped dramatically because they are poached for caviar
5	Goldenseal	A herb found in hardwood forests in North America. Now rare because of high demand for use as a healing herb
6	Alligator snapping turtle	Largest turtle in North America. Heavily hunted for its meat, which is sold around the world
7	Hawksbill turtle	Found mainly around tropical reefs. At serious risk because of illegal killing for its beautiful shell
8	Big leaf mahogany	Found in tropical forests in central and South America. Perhaps 70 per cent of world's supply has been cut down for its red-coloured wood
9	Green-cheeked parrot	Natural habitat is in Mexico. Now rare because many captured and sold as pets, even though this is now illegal
10	Mako shark	Widely hunted for its fins, used in shark fin soup. Fishing boats often cut off the fins and throw rest of shark back in the sea

Deforestation rates around the world

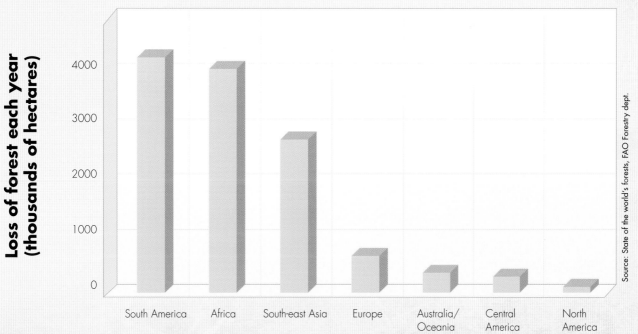

Loss of forest each year (thousands of hectares)

4000
3000
2000
1000
0

South America · Africa · South-east Asia · Europe · Australia/Oceania · Central America · North America

Source: State of the world's forests, FAO Forestry dept.

GLOSSARY

acid rain
rain that has been made more acid than normal by air pollution

aquifer
an underground layer of rock that contains water

asthma
an illness in which people have trouble breathing

barren
without life

biodiversity
the variety of animals and plants in an area

bioethanol
a biofuel that can be used instead of petrol

blight
when an area of land has been ruined by an activity such as mining

carbon emissions
gases containing carbon, released when a fuel is burned, for example

CFCs (chlorofluorocarbons)
chemicals that were once used in aerosol sprays and fridges, which can make holes in the ozone layer

climate
the average weather of a region over a period of many years

climate change
the gradual changes in the overall weather of the whole planet

contaminate
to pollute by something impure

diabetes
an illness in which the body cannot properly control sugar levels in the blood

dioxins
polluting gases that can cause cancer in humans. These gases are produced when certain substances are burned

ecosystem
all the living things in area, together with the landscape and climate conditions in the area

eroded
worn away by wind and water

fertiliser
a substance (usually chemical) added to soil or water to increase the amount of crops it can produce

fossil fuels
the natural fuels found in the Earth's crust, formed from the remains of living organisms

glacier
a frozen river of ice

greenhouse gas
a gas in the atmosphere that traps some of the Sun's heat

habitat
the environment that a plant or animal lives in

herbicide
a mix of chemicals used to kill unwanted weeds

hydroelectricity
electricity generated by the action of running water

irrigation
the artificial watering of farm crops

LEDCs
less economically developed (poorer) countries

MEDCs
more economically developed (richer) countries

microbes
tiny living things too small to see without a microscope

minerals
substances such as metals, precious stones, oil, coal and salt, which are found in the Earth's surface and mined

multiple sclerosis
a disease of the nervous system in which a person gradually becomes weaker and loses muscle control

nitrates
chemical compounds that contain nitrogen and oxygen

ore
rock containing high concentrations of metals or other useful resources

over-exploiting
using up too many resources

over-graze
allowing cattle, goats or sheep to eat too much grass in an area

ozone
a special form of oxygen

Parkinson's disease
a disease of the brain that causes locked or trembling muscles, loss of balance and difficulty with walking

pesticides
chemicals that kill insect pests

phytoplankton
plant-like microscopic creatures found in the oceans

photosynthesis
a chemical process in green plants and some micro-organisms, during which carbon dioxide is absorbed and oxygen is released

pollution
the effect of poisonous or harmful substances that are released into the environment

quota
in the fishing industry, an amount of fish that a fishing boat is allowed to catch, set by the government

reserves
the amount of a natural resource that is left

reservoir
an artificial lake

sediment
small particles of rock such as sand, silt or mud

smelting
heating an ore to extract the metal from it

smog
a kind of haze or fog caused by air pollution

species
a group of related animals or plants

spoil
in mining, the waste left over after the valuable materials have been extracted from rocks

sulphates
chemical compounds that contain sulphur and oxygen

switchgrass
a tall grass that was once the main kind of grass on the American prairies

toxic
something that is poisonous

vulnerable
people who are more at risk than others

water table
the level of below ground at which you can find water

worked out
a mine that has been worked out no longer has any minerals or metals remaining in it

FURTHER READING

Air Pollution (21st Century Debates) by Matthew Chapman and Rob Bowden (Hodder Wayland, 2001)

Biodiversity by E. O. Wilson (National Academy Press, 1988)

Biodiversity (Global Issues) by Cheryl Jakab (Smart Apple Media, 2008)

Bloomin' Rainforests (Horrible Geography) by Anita Ganeri (Hippo, 2001)

Fossil Fuels (Energy Sources) by Neil Morris (Franklin Watts, 2006)

Rocks and Soil (Our Earth) by Jen Green (PowerKids Books, 2008)

Saving the Rainforests by Sally Morgan (Franklin Watts, 2005)

Thirsty World by Steve Parker (Heinemann, 2003)

INDEX

WEBFINDER

www.enviroliteracy.org/
Learn more about biodiversity, ecosystems, water use and energy on this excellent website

www.blueplanetbiomes.org/rainforest.htm
Learn about the plants and animals that live in the world's rainforests

http://ga.water.usgs.gov/edu/mearth.html
Where is the Earth's water? How much is there? Learn the answers to these and other water questions

http://na.unep.net/OnePlanetManyPeople/index.php
The United Nations report on how human actions are damaging our world